Winchester Public Library
Winchester, MA 01890
781-721-7171
www.winpublib.org

Published in 2013 by The Rosen Publishing Group, Inc.
29 East 21st Street, New York, NY 10010

Photo Credits: **KEY** tl=top left; tc=top center; tr=top right; cl=center left; c=center; cr=center right; bl=bottom left; bc=bottom center; br=bottom right; bg=background

CBT = Corbis; DT = Dreamstime; GI = Getty Images; iS = istockphoto.com; SH = Shutterstock; TF = Topfoto; TP = photolibrary.com; wiki = Wikipedia

1c iS; **2–3**tc TF; **4–5**cl SH; **6**bc SH; **6–7**bg iS; c, c SH; **7**tr SH; **8**tr CBT; bc, bl, br, tr iS; c SH; cl, cr TF; **9**bl, tl, tr iS; tl, tr TF; cl TPL; **13**br iS; **14**bl SH; **14–15**bc iS; **15**br iS; c SH; **16**bc iS; tr SH; **16–17** tc iS; **17**tr GI; bc SH; cr TF; **18**bl, **18–19**; **20–21**bc TF; **21**tr SH; tc TF; **22**bc wiki; **22–23**bg iS; **23**tr CBT; bl, tl SH; br TF; **24–25**cl SH; **25**br DT; **26**tr DT; bl iS; **26–27**tc DT; **27**c SH; **28**cl SH; c, cr TF; **28–29**c, tc TF; **29**tr iS; cr SH; tc TF; **30–31**bg iS; **31**br, c SH

All illustrations copyright Weldon Owen Pty Ltd. Lionel Portier

Weldon Owen Pty Ltd
Managing Director: Kay Scarlett
Creative Director: Sue Burk
Publisher: Helen Bateman
Senior Vice President, International Sales: Stuart Laurence
Vice President Sales North America: Ellen Towell
Administration Manager, International Sales: Kristine Ravn

Library of Congress Cataloging-in-Publication Data
Einspruch, Andrew.
 Wired world / by Andrew Einspruch. — 1st ed.
   p. cm. — (Discovery education: technology)
 Includes index.
 ISBN 978-1-4488-7888-8 (library binding) — ISBN 978-1-4488-7970-0 (pbk.) —
 ISBN 978-1-4488-7976-2 (6-pack)
 1. Telecommunication—Juvenile literature. 2. Information technology—Juvenile literature. I. Title.
 TK5102.4.E46 2013
 303.48'33—dc23
                    2011051641

Manufactured in the United States of America

CPSIA Compliance Information: Batch #SW12PK: For Further Information contact Rosen Publishing, New York, New York at 1-800-237-9932

Discovery
EDUCATION

TECHNOLOGY

WIRED WORLD

ANDREW EINSPRUCH

PowerKiDS press.

New York

Contents

Always Connected, Doing Everything

We live in a connected world. Our modern lives are characterized by people and devices, such as computers and phones, that are constantly connected to each other or, at most, a few moments away from that connection. We share data, information, and knowledge continually and almost instantaneously.

Sometimes, what we share is a small tidbit, such as where we are or what we want for lunch. Sometimes, it is meaningful, analytical, full of feeling, or the one piece of information that might save a life. The miracle of modern technology is that it lets us be as connected to each other and to information as we want to be.

Home desktop computer
Computers in the home first became popular in the 1980s. Today, there are millions of them, and almost all are connected to the Internet. Essential for accessing information and fostering connections among people, they are also increasingly important sources of entertainment.

That's Amazing!

As of 2010, it was estimated that there were more than 4.6 billion cell phone subscriptions in use worldwide. That is up from just 12 million 10 years before.

Smart phone

A smart phone is less of a phone and more of a computer in your pocket that also handles calls and text messages. Smart phones can do many of the same things a full-sized computer can, such as e-mail and Internet surfing.

ATM withdrawal

Automatic teller machines (ATMs) are perfect examples of the modern, connected world. You can use almost any ATM in the world and, through connections made possible by modern communication, find out your account balance and withdraw money.

Communication Before Electricity

P eople have always communicated with each other. Language and song date back a million years or so. The difficulty was always how to communicate over a distance that was beyond the human voice. We can shout only so loud and for so long.

From early on, people explored different ways to communicate from farther and farther apart. Some methods, such as drumming or bugling, used sound. Others were visual, such as smoke signals, semaphore, and signal lamps. In either case, these methods extended the reach and speed of human communication.

Town crier
Back when most people could not read or write, town criers were the first newscasters. They would ring a bell, call "Oyez, oyez, oyez," then read an official statement from the king, deliver news, or publicize official proclamations, such as market days or new laws.

Smoke signals
Smoke signals were used by the Native Americans and the Chinese. A fire was built, green grass or branches were added to create smoke, and a blanket was used to control the shape and size of the smoke puffs as well as the length of time between them.

African drums
These were useful for communicating in forested areas, where sound worked better than visual messages. "Talking drums" conveyed messages by mimicking the tone of an actual language, as well as the length of its syllables, and the stress of its words.

Military bugle call
The bugle was an effective way to communicate with soldiers. Different bugle calls told the soldiers what they needed to do at different time of the day, such as get up, eat, assemble to work, or go to bed. Recorded bugle calls are still used today.

Church bells
The ringing of church bells would convey simple messages, such as "Come to prayer" or "Gather quickly, there is an emergency." The message could be varied by changing the number of times the bell was rung or the type of bell used.

Semaphore
Different positions and combinations of flags or lights were used to convey information. This information might be prearranged meanings or letters of the alphabet. By using semaphore, along with telescopes to see them, messages could be received over distances of many miles.

Written messages
Since they did not have to be interpreted or relayed, written messages had the advantage of being able to communicate complex ideas faithfully. They were slow, however, because they had to be physically carried from one place to another.

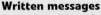

Signal lamps and lanterns
Signal lights were an important means of communication at night, especially for ships. Signal lamps were used from the 1800s, and complex messages could be sent by using flashes of light to represent the dots and dashes of Morse code.

Communication with Electricity

Harnessing electrical power completely changed the way people connect with each other. The first demonstration of the telegraph occurred in 1837 and, within a few decades, a message that would have taken months to cross half the planet by boat could be transmitted in a matter of moments. In the years that followed, speeds increased, as did the length of messages sent and the ease with which they were transmitted.

With tools such as phones, e-mail, and instant messaging (IM), communication today is virtually instantaneous, irrespective of whether you are in the same building or completely across the globe.

Telegraph
The telegraph was the first technology to link people all over the world with almost instantaneous communication. It was based on sending messages in Morse code, long and short pulses of electricity that are grouped together to represent letters and numbers.

Telephone
The telephone took the idea of the telegraph and added voice and immediate two-way communication. Invented in the 1870s, telephones soon brought conversation at a distance to millions of people. In the United States alone, between 1894 and 1904, the number of phones grew from 285,000 to 3,317,000.

Radio
The first form of wireless communication technology, radio was a broadcast, a one-way medium that allowed a single message, or program, to reach a huge number of people. The first broadcast was in 1906. Within eight decades, there were 12,000 radio stations in the United States.

Movies
Similar to television and radio, movies are a form of one-way communication. In the early years, though, they were not just about telling stories through film. Until the 1950s, movie theaters also screened newsreels, short documentaries that gave news reports.

Television

Television emerged in the 1950s and 1960s. While radio first brought mass communication into the home, television transformed it into a visual medium. As it communicated news and entertainment, the television soon became a focal point of the average home.

Satellite

Communication satellites made it possible to connect to remote parts of the world not connected to the wired phone network. Originally used for long-distance telephone calls, they now carry other communications, such as television programs and Internet data.

Computer network

Using readily accessible computers found in homes and offices, computer networks gave people the chance to connect to a vast web of information, entertainment, and images. Since its beginnings in the 1990s, the Internet has opened up a world of information.

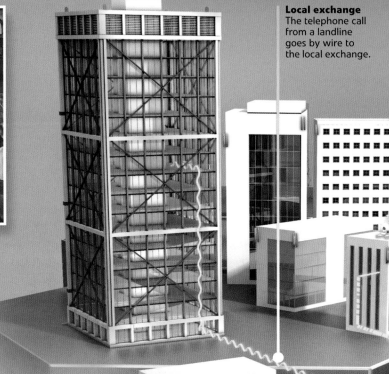

Local exchange
The telephone call from a landline goes by wire to the local exchange.

Manual exchange
Before computers and electronic equipment, all telephone calls were manually connected by telephone operators, who were almost always women. The operator made a physical connection between the wires of the two phone lines involved in the call.

How a Telephone Call Works

A telephone call starts with a voice saying something at one end and ends with an ear hearing it at the other. In between, there is a massive amount of technology that converts the voice into an electrical signal, passes that signal over a wire, optic fiber, or a radio wave to the destination phone, and converts it back into something that can be heard.

Given that there are billions of phones on the planet, one of the most important parts of the call takes place at the telephone exchange. This is where the electrical signals of the phone call are routed from one place to another, ultimately connecting to the correct destination number.

Routing a call
Phone calls are transmitted by combination of radio waves a wires or optic fibers. The signa is sent from the local exchang or cell phone tower to a main exchange, then ultimately bac to a local exchange and the destination phone number.

Main exchange
It is then transferred from the local exchange to the region's main telephone exchange.

Between main exchanges
The call then goes to a destination main exchange that covers the area of the destination telephone.

Cell tower
This receives calls from cell phones and routes them to a mobile exchange.

Mobile signal
A cell phone transmits call signals to the closest cell tower.

The world's telephone system handles several billion calls and texts a day between 4.6 billion cell phones and 1.3 billion landlines.

Modern telephone system
Compared to the original, manual telephone exchange, today's computer-based exchanges can handle a great deal more lines and calls simultaneously. These modern systems are smaller, cost less, and do much more than the equipment that came before them.

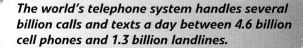

?... You Decide

t used to be that all telephones were a fixed landline, that is, tethered by a wire to a particular place. Today, the vast majority of telephones are cell phones. These can be taken almost anywhere and associate a phone number to a person instead of a place. Which is better—landline or cell phone?

Landline

Landline telephones connect to the phone system by wires or optic fibers. They are associated with a fixed place, such as a home or business, and sometimes even a spot within that place, for example, the living room or reception area. Landline call tend to be cheaper than cell phone calls.

Standard telephone

These do one thing well—making telephone calls between places. The handset and the base of the telephone are connected by wires, which means they stay in one place all the time.

Cell phone

A cell phone can be used anywhere that is in range of a cell phone tower. Unlike a landline, it is not associated with a particular place. Cell phones provide greater freedom, but usually cost more to use.

ing photos

ost all modern cell phones have a number on-phone features built into them. The most mon is a camera, which takes still pictures. e have video as well. This means that almost yone now carries a camera with them.

E-mails and web surfing

Smart phones are able to transfer data as well as phone signals. This means that they give the user the ability to surf the Internet, check e-mails, and other actions that require the movement of data.

rdless phone

ordless phone uses a dline connection to the ephone network, but gives eater mobility by using dio waves to connect the andset to the base station, which controls the calls. The andset must stay within adio range of the base unit.

Smart Phones

In essence, smart phones are pocket-sized computers. The difference between them and regular cell phones is their ability to interact with the Internet. They access and transmit data, giving the user full access to functions such as e-mail, web surfing, instant messaging, and social networking. Of course, they also have the features people expect in a regular cell phone, such as a camera, text messaging, and the ability to make phone calls.

Smart phones usually have some sort of keyboard, either a physical one or a simulated one that relies on a touch screen. This lets users enter text more easily than a standard phone keypad can.

Maps

Most smart phones have access to maps, making it easier for users to find their way around a location. These maps can tell where the phone is and, using that knowledge, provide customized directions to a specified destination.

Social networking

Social network sites, such as Twitter and Facebook, give people a way to stay connected with friends and acquaintances. Smart phones provide easy access to these social sites, recognizing that people like to connect with them while on the go.

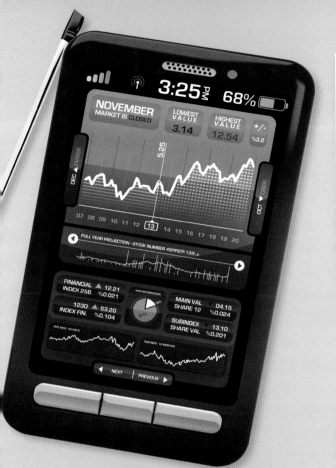

Gaming

Playing games on smart phones is booming in popularity. The devices now have better power and screen clarity, so it is possible to create compelling games for them. Many of these games are motion sensitive, detecting phone movement as part of game play.

nking

nt to check your bank account balance while you are away
n your computer? Smart phones let you use Internet banking
n your phone, either through a dedicated application or
ough a mobile web interface.

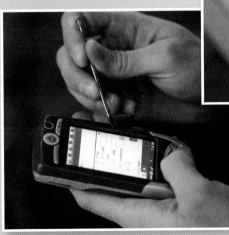

sonal digital assistant

rt phones can help you
track of personal and
ness details. They can
appointments using a
ndar function, as well as
contact details so you
ot need a separate
ress book.

Surfing the web

If it is on the Internet, the odds are good that your smart phone can help you see it. Many websites detect if they are being viewed using a smart phone, and change what is displayed to accommodate the screen size.

Connecting Everything

The Internet is only a few decades old, but it has completely transformed the world. The connecting of computers and free sharing of information has opened up a world of possibilities. It has changed the way we communicate, how we get our news, share our lives, and stay in touch with friends and family.

The World Wide Web, or the "www" that is part of a web address, is even newer. Web pages use a particular type of format, called HTML, for presenting information to the screen. HTML was created in 1990, so every web page you will ever see has been created since then.

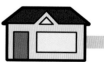

Home

How it works

Connecting to the Internet rec using a computer to transmit receive data. That data move: through any number of conne computer networks until you the information you want.

Corporation

7 Online content

The user's computer communicates via the Interne with other computers to acce the online content they hold (such as Web pages, video, audio, and e-mail).

BUILT TO WITHSTAND A BOMB

Part of the original reason for the Internet was the US military's desire to keep control of bombers and missiles, even if a nuclear bomb exploded. The solution was to decentralize the control. If any part of the network disappeared, other parts would automatically choose new routes around the problem area.

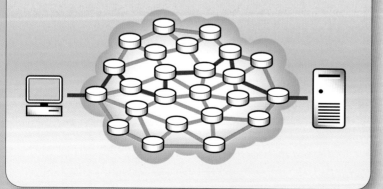

Computer 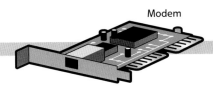 Modem  Firewall

er's computer
n home and business
puters connect to the
net, they help you reach
ge amount of information
ed online.

2 Communication equipment
The computer connects to the
Internet using communication
equipment like a modem, network
interface card, local area network
(LAN), and/or a router.

3 Firewall
The computer or LAN will have
a protective firewall to keep
the computer safe from
intrusions from the Internet.

Computer   LAN    Firewall

4 Local loop carrier
This connects the user to
the Internet over a wire
(provided by a cable TV,
phone, or electricity
company), or by satellite
or wireless connection.

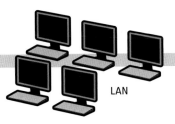

P backbone
ISP backbone connects
ISP (and users connected
) to other ISPs. Massive
unts of data move across
e high-speed backbones.

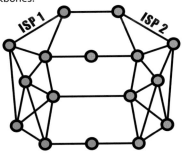

ISP 1   ISP 2

5 ISP
The Internet Service
Provider (ISP) provides
customers with access
to the Internet,
facilitating the Internet
connection and
routing data.

ISP

Why Be Wired?

Most people would not even consider asking the question, "Is it worth being connected to the Internet?" For most of us, it is simply a fact of modern life. Nevertheless, it is a question worth thinking about.

Being connected to the Internet provides us with a huge variety of information. This might be news as it is happening, or access to the wealth of knowledge on websites. This wired (and wireless) connection gives us more flexibility in our choices, more mobility in our movements, and the chance for a real-time connection to friends, coworkers, and family, no matter where they are on the planet.

Multiplayer games

One reason to live a wired life is because it is fun. For example, multiplayer online games give people a chance to explore virtual worlds while participating in activities that involve interacting with people who may be next doc or on the other side of the world.

REAL-TIME COMMUNICATION

Thanks to the Internet, the way we communicate is changing. We expect our communication to be much faster and always available. For example, e-mail gives us the ability to send the equivalent of a letter to anyone who has an e-mail address, and we have the expectation that it will arrive within moments.

Letters
These can take days, even weeks, to be delivered. A letter from the UK to Australia sent 150 years ago took months to arrive by ship.

Instant messaging
IM, or instant messaging, serves the same function as letters, but, where letter delivery is measured in days, IM delivery is in seconds, or even fractions of a second.

Innovation in a Wired World

As devices and people become increasingly connected, new uses are continually being developed. Remote-controlled cameras, for example, allow for observation at a distance. This is useful for scientists who want to observe animals in the wild, but can also be used by security forces. Remote devices that perform functions, such as turning systems on and off, can be monitored with these kinds of remote cameras.

Internet telephony, online chat, and video conferencing give people the chance to interact while staying at home or in the office. This is useful for friends and family, but also has applications for people needing medical or technical consultations.

Remote security
Security robots can help authorities keep an eye on what is happening in public areas. They transmit video and audio to a remote location, and can move from place to place on their own.

INNOVATION IN A WIRED WORLD

nline consultation

al-time chats and video conferences are
rfect for remote contact with help desk
nsultants and job candidates. Video
teraction provides an experience that is
ose to being there in person, allowing
vo-way conversation and visual feedback.

Remote surgery

High-speed video technology and surgical
robots are helping surgeons perform on
patients who need their specialist skills.
They remove the need for the doctor and
patient to travel to the same place, but still
deliver a superior quality of surgical care.

hristmas lights

fun way of using digital interactivity
Christmas light displays that can be
ontrolled over the Internet. Random
ternet surfers drop by websites that
now these displays, and use online
otions to control which lights are active.

Webcam science research

Cameras that transmit images and sounds
across the Internet are called webcams.
These let scientists continuously monitor
remote locations, observing and recording
animal behavior over much longer periods
than is possible with live field observation.

Parental supervision

A key to online safety is parents knowing what their children are doing. While children often know more about the technical side of things, parents know more about how people behave and how to stay safe in online environments.

Staying Safe in a Wired World

One of the great things about living in a wired world is the openness it creates through the ability to share information from around the world. But this openness also means you must be careful because it is easy for people to pretend to be someone or something they are not.

Staying safe is simple, but requires awareness, caution, and some effort. The most important things to remember are installing security software on your computer and setting it to automatically stay up to date, changing passwords often and keeping them hard to guess, not posting personal details online, and not opening attachments unless you are certain they are safe.

Did You Know?

many people use easy-to-guess passwords. Some to avoid are ny sequential string of numbers, password," "qwerty," "letmein," ur pet's name, or your birth date.

Online chat rooms
Never give out personal details to people you do not know. Even snippets of information, such as the name of your school, hobbies and interests, or your general location are all pieces in a puzzle that someone could put together to identify you personally.

Crime in a Wired World

Where there is money or valuable information, there will be people who want to steal it. This is as true in the online world as it is in the real world. Criminals have moved online, adopting a range of methods that let them collect your valuable information to use for fraudulent purposes.

Some criminals use computer technology to break into secured and unsecured online databases to get what they are looking for. Others simply trick people into giving up useful personal details, such as passwords and account numbers, which they then exploit. Some criminals use a combination of the two.

Credit cards
Stolen credit card information is used to make unauthorized purchases by phone or online. Thieves get this information from hacked computers, dishonest retailers who sell the information, and from discarded credit card statements and receipts.

Shopping online
If done safely, shopping onlin can be a great experience. Bu only from reputable, known companies who use secure websites. Many people get a credit card to use only for on shopping and keep it at a low maximum-purchase amount.

...ming

...bank cards are read by an
...onic reader that collects the
...nation stored in the magnetic
...on the back, without the card
...r's knowledge, this is called
...ning. Skimming might be
...with a device attached to an
...or by a shop assistant who
...a separate reader.

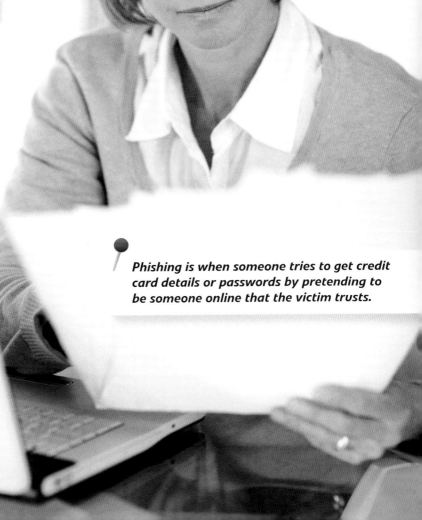

...king statements

...ing your bank statements for
...pected charges is an important
...f making sure your credit card
...being used fraudulently. Not
...gal transactions are for large
...nts—some criminals specialize
...all dollar transactions, hoping
...will slip by unnoticed.

Phishing is when someone tries to get credit card details or passwords by pretending to be someone online that the victim trusts.

Time Line to a Wired World

The Internet and our wired world did not appear magically overnight. They were, in fact, built on technology that evolved over hundreds of years in a steady progression, piling innovation on top of innovation. Some of these were huge leaps forward, such as the Internet itself. Others, such as moving from black-and-white to color TV, were smaller steps.

These innovations have brought us to today's connected world, where many people and information are no more than a few moments away, anywhere in the world.

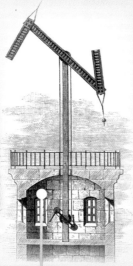

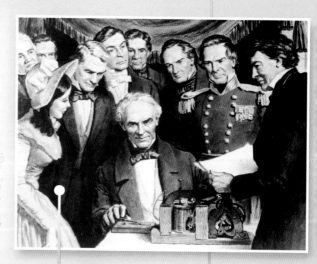

From 700 BC
For many years, the fastest, most reliable form of communication was a message delivered by carrier pigeon. These birds were trained to fly to known locations with messages strapped to their legs.

1792
The first semaphore messages were relayed with a series of semaphore towers designed by Claude Chappe, linking Paris and Lille, in France. The two-armed devices were posted on towers 20 miles (32 km) apart.

1844
The first public demonstration of Samuel Morse's electric telegraph occurred on May 24, 1844. The first message, sent between Washington, D.C., and Baltimore was, "What hath God wrought."

1876
The first successful telephone call was made on March 10, 1876 by the Scotsman Alexander Graham Bell to his assistant, Thomas Watson. The words he spoke were, "Come here, Watson. I want you.

1927
John Logie Baird
transmitted a TV signal
over a distance of
428 miles (705 km), from
London to Glasgow, UK,
across a phone line. The
next year, his company
sent a TV image from
London to New York.

1970
Researchers at Corning
Glass Works created a
glass fiber capable of
transmitting light. These
fibers revolutionized
communication by hugely
increasing the speed and
distance of data transfer
compared to electricity.

1992
On December 3, 1992,
Neil Papworth sent the first
text message, "Merry
Christmas," to the phone
of Richard Jarvis. By the
end of the decade, this
inexpensive communication
method exploded to billions
of messages every year.

was first demonstrated
uglielmo Marconi,
alian (above). He
mitted radio signals
nd 1 mile (1.6 km).
Russian Alexander
novich Popov
onstrated a radio
er that same year.

Glossary

ATM (ay-tee-EM) Short for "automatic teller machine," this device confirms a person's bank account details and dispenses cash.

cell phone (SEL FOHN) Also called a mobile phone, this transportable radio device enables two-way conversations without wired handsets. It is associated with a person rather than a location.

communications equipment (kuh-myoo-nih-KAY-shunz ih-KWIP-ment) Electronic equipment that facilitates the transmission and reception of data between people and organizations.

computer network (kum-PYOO-ter NET-wurk) A collection of connected computers that share data.

data (DAY-tuh) Information that is manipulated and stored by computers.

exchange (iks-CHAYNJ) A telecommunications facility where lines from telephones are connected.

firewall (FYR-wahl) Protective software that prevents malicious and undesirable access to a computer.

HTML (aych-tee-em-EL) Short for "hypertext markup language," this is the standard language used for creating web pages on the Internet.

information (in-fer-MAY-shun) Data that has been organized and interpreted to have meaning.

instant messages (IM) (IN-stint MEH-sij-ez) Short, text-based messages that are delivered more or less instantly.

Internet (IN-ter-net) A worldwide network of connected computers that can share data.

Internet telephony (IN-ter-net teh-LEH-fuh-nee) Phone calls placed over the Internet. It is also called VoIP, or Voice over Internet Protocol.

knowledge (NAW-lij) Organized information used to create expertise and skill.

landline (LAND-lyn) A telephone connected to the phone network by wires, and associated with a fixed locatio[n]

Morse code (MORS KOHD) A telegraph code, invented by Samuel Morse, that uses short dots and longer dashes to represent the letters of the alphabet.

phishing (FISH-ing) Trying to trick someone into revealing personal details, suc[h] as credit card information or passwords, that can then be u[sed] for illegal purposes.

radio (RAY-dee-oh) A broadcast medium that communicates by sending electrical signals wirelessly through the air.

real–time communication (REEL-ty[m] kuh-myoo-nih-KAY-shun) Communication that happens the moment, rather than bein[g] delayed. A phone conversatio[n] is real-time communication, while a newspaper is not.

satellite (SA-tih-lyt) A communications device that resides in space and relays communication signals to different points on Earth.

emaphore (SEH-muh-for)
communications system that
ses flag or lantern positions to
epresent letters of the alphabet
short messages.

ignal lamps (SIG-nul
AMPS) Lights used to send
ded messages at night.

kimming (SKIM-ing) Using a
evice to read information from a
nk or credit card so it can
used illegally.

mart phone (SMART FOHN)
small, portable computer
at, in addition to making
one calls, can access the
ternet and transmit and
ceive data.

cial networking
H-shul NET-wurk-ing)
e use of online systems,
ch as Twitter and Facebook,
connect and share with
ends and acquaintances.

egraph (TEH-lih-graf)
evice that uses electrical
ses, not voice signals,
t by wire to communicate
er a distance.

ephone (TEH-lih-fohn)
wo-way communications
vice that originally relied on
dsets connected by wires.

television (TEH-lih-vih-zhen)
A broadcast medium that
transmits sound and images
wirelessly through the air, and
now also via cables under
the ground.

touch screen (TUCH SKREEN)
A screen, often found on smart
phones, that is sensitive to touch
and uses the user's touch as a
form of input.

town crier (TOWN CRY-er)
An official who called out
statements from governing
authorities and delivered news in
the days before mass media.

webcam (WEB-kam) A camera
set up to transmit its images
across the Internet. The images
are often available for the public
to view.

Index

Websites

Due to the changing nature of Internet links, PowerKids Press has developed an online list of websites related to the subject of this book. This site is updated regularly. Please use this link to access the list: www.powerkidslinks.com/disc/wired/